SUBMISSION TO MASTER

IN SEARCH OF MAN'S AUTHENTIC NATURE

Jim Von Schounmacher

Published by Daniele Luciano Moskal
UNIQUE WRITING PUBICATIONS
PO BOX 582, Waltham Cross,
Herts, EN8 1AU, England.

First Edition 2008
Second Edition 2015
Third Edition 2019

DEDICATION

This book is dedicated to:

My daughter Hope Annalina and my beloved wife Catherine, for their undying love and support.

And to:

David Hancock McCombs, my friend and mentor, Charles S. Labatt and Roberto "Onesimus" Valenzuela whose Godly influence has changed me forever.

And a special thanks to Christine Shoemaker

In loving memory...
"Miss Leah"
May 1, 1981 ~ February 18, 2009

CONTENTS

FOREWORD BY THE PUBLISHER

The Holy Bible in the Book of Genesis, the book of 'first beginnings' states clearly that GOD is the Creator, the Maker of Heaven and Earth. HE is the Essence from which all Truth and Knowledge emanates. HE is the One who is above and beyond our finite minds. HE is the Infinite One. HIS might is so great that HE made both the sun and the atom. HIS might is so controlled that HE made the things only microscopes reveal. HIS might is so complete that HE delicately put the dust on the butterfly's wings.

Just like a thoroughbred horse GOD is unbelievably strong yet supremely gentle. HE is amazingly powerful, yet touchingly loving. HE is the Giver of Life, the LORD of Nature, and the GOD of all Creation, the Great Redeemer, and the Author of Salvation. NO ONE is greater, and certainly no one is mightier than HE!

I am happy to commend this excellent book. It is a fine piece of work from a new American Author, Pastor and Texas Cowboy, Jim Von Schounmacher who has humbly attempted to further exalt the Name of the GOD of Israel, whom we have known and loved, proved and worshipped, followed and served, down the years. By using his expertise with horses to teach us about GOD's principles of "Submission to a Master", in a very easy-to-comprehend way, Jim explains how the mastery of a big and powerful, wild and un-tamed horse is broken into, and how GOD takes us in the palm of HIS mighty and tender hands and slowly but surely begins to melt us, mold us, shape us, discipline and disciple us for HIS glory!

The photographs included, which are singularly beautiful, will also provide the reader with endless pleasure and profit and an insight into how GOD demonstrates HIS truth and HIS principles of submission through these majestic creations… HIS horses.

~ Daniele Luciano Moskal ~

(UNIQUE WRITING PUBLICATIONS)

Unless otherwise indicated, all Scriptures quotations used in this book are taken from the New American Standard Bible version (NASB) copyright © 1971, 1995 of the Holy Bible. Used by permission of Zondervan Publishing House

INTRODUCTION

In 1995 I met David McCombs in Grand Lake, Colorado... that meeting changed my life. "Winding River Ranch" is the place I first met Dave McCombs a man I hold dear as a friend, a mentor and a Pastor... Dave McCombs is a unique individual... he's a cowboy at heart and comes by that naturally, his granddad, Dallas McCombs, "The meanest little man in Texas," was a Texas Ranger.

Dave lives in a county up in Northwest Texas... Colorado, Parker, Colorado to be exact. His horses and his dogs are a special part of his life. But they don't hold a candle to his life's mate and wife Judy or the grandchildren. Dave has served the LORD most of his life. He began with Campus Crusade for CHRIST in 1974. And with Dr. Bright's blessing several years ago left Campus to deliver a message that he has developed and fine tuned for more than 15 years through diligent research, field tests and a whole lot of prayer.

I found his message to be as unique as its deliverer... focusing on masculine authenticity as evidenced in the Scriptures. He is a speaker, writer, and a motivator... but most of all he is a mighty man of GOD and I am blest to count him my friend. Dave is a man you can trust to tell you what you need to hear... and it will always line up with the Word of GOD. The message GOD has given him is for "a time such as this!"

Dave is a quiet cowboy that has the Spirit of GOD all over him… he had been with Campus Crusade For Christ for some 25 years when we met and had spent years developing a men's ministry that addressed the critical lack of understanding of men as to what GOD requires of them. Man's Authentic Nature (M.A.N.) was designed to offer men the opportunity to "trade up" for a new and authentic experience of masculine freedom and power.

David's mission was that of "Male Restoration." Helping men restore themselves to a right relationship with GOD, with themselves and with others. David and I must have been cast out of the same mold… or as the word of GOD says... we were created for "a time such as this." David put in words things that I knew but had never expressed. At the conclusion of our first encounter I knew GOD had sent David to put me on the path HE had chosen for me. And everything that has transpired since has proven that to be true. I believe with all my heart that the overall effectiveness of all men in ministry is dependent upon the internalization of an authentic masculine relationship with GOD.

My best friend and wife put my meeting Dave this way... "My husband Jim has grown immeasurably through his association with David McCombs and M.A.N. Ministries. David's vision and his faithful adherence to GOD's calling on his life have been a blessing as well as an awesome example. I applaud this book and recommend it to every man who desires to learn more about being the Biblical man GOD ordained him to be. As a wife and mother I thank GOD for you David... Jim is a better husband, father and pastor than ever before."

GOD brought Dave and I together because "iron sharpens iron" and together we have a message that HE has prepared to change your future forever. I encourage you to read this book with a heart that seeks to allow Man's Authentic Nature to be apart of your life as I did mine... I assure you, you will never be the same.

Back in the early 90's "Esquire" magazine did a feature article on the modern men's movement in

America. As part of their coverage, they invited 50 or so nationally prominent women to submit 100 word essays on men and their movement.

Esquire took those essays and the commentary of many women in political and corporate leadership and summarized them as follows:

"Men are not fit to lead. If we could put them in cages, maintain a group for reproductive purposes, and fill all power and influence positions with women, we could eliminate political struggle, economic struggle, war, hunger, greed, crime, poverty and all the other evils of the world's societies. These problems are rooted in the ego of the male. His self-centered competitive nature, his desire to assert himself over others, his hardness and the insidious fear that rules his life is the curse of history."

The sad story is this sad story is true. Man has been leading the world astray since the beginning of time. So how do we change that dynamic... how do we solve this problem?

We begin by acknowledging that we can't solve this problem... but for the transforming power and influence of the **LORD JESUS CHRIST** we can do nothing.

So where do we begin? An Ancient axiom states: *"A journey of a thousand miles begins with but a single step!"* But, a single step... we must draw a line in the sand and say "No More!" and that will require, as Paul states in Romans 12:2... *"A renewing of your mind..."*

We must understand and accept the sovereignty of

God. Saying you know that GOD is sovereign and accepting that GOD is sovereign are two completely separate things.

We men far too often express understanding of things we haven't the foggiest notion about. As men we always want to appear to be in the "know".

I have said all that to say this…the things of GOD are not discernable by our limited finite minds. They emanate from the unlimited, infinite mind of GOD. Still we men continue to try, in vain, to paint GOD into a box with parameters that we can define, explain and understand. But sadly that always leads to wrong conclusions and spiritual chaos.

To discern the things of GOD we must rely on the HOLY SPIRIT to give us wisdom and understanding. That discernment only comes with total submission to GOD. Both intellectually acknowledging HIM as GOD and emotionally accepting HIM as LORD in your life. HE is the boss and has final say in all things.

But instead you and I want to understand the "BIG Picture", as we in Texas would say, "The Whole Enchilada!" We want details, we want a plan and we want to work the plan and see results. To us, seeing is believing. But GOD says, HE has a plan and if we will just believe we will see. But to do it HIS way requires FAITH.

But what is FAITH? If I were to ask a dozen theologians to define faith, I would no doubt get twelve wonderfully insightful profound responses. All doctrinally accurate, similar in content, but subtly different. FAITH is one of those things that ONLY the infinite unlimited mind of GOD can truly define. And we are blest… because HE did… just for us HE personally gave us HIS definition of FAITH.

In Hebrews 11:6 we read:

"And without faith, it is impossible to please God for he who comes to God must know that He is…" (Hebrews 11:6)

Know that HE is what? We must know that HE is GOD… HIS definition could not be more clear. Faith is knowing GOD is GOD… not knowing HE is a god… but knowing HE is the GOD. When you arrive at that understanding you can rejoice in the assurance that the GOD of all creation has a plan for your life, it is a plan to give you a future and a hope, it is a plan in which HE causes all things to work together for good to those who love HIM. Once that truth sinks into your mind and thought process… your life will change forever.

Knowing GOD is GOD requires believing HIS word is true and acting accordingly. The profundity of that revelation will open your heart and mind to desire, above all, to please HIM and become the man of GOD you have been called to be. That transformation will overwhelm you with joy and fulfillment.

In 1836 one hundred and forty seven men gathered in a

place called the Alamo. One night Colonel William Barret Travis took his saber and drew a line in the sand, He offered the men with him a choice.

Those who would step across that line would do so knowing it meant certain death... and in doing so they changed the face of history forever.

Today you are being offered the opportunity to change your future forever... to take a step across the line from believer to knower. It is a step that will mean certain death. The old man will die and you will find a new life walking hand in hand with the HOLY SPIRIT of GOD. But an invitation is all you will get... the rest is up to you. HE is standing with open arms... you can accept HIS hand or keep on wandering blind... HE waits for you to step across the line.

Back in my youth a teacher told me that I could never acquire too much knowledge... she said, "Knowledge is strength." When I repeated that bit of wisdom to my father in an attempt to impress him, he responded, "Knowledge is strength... but correct application of that strength is POWER!"

If you open your hearts and minds today GOD is about to use HIS creations, these majestic horses, to give you insights and understanding to the masculine Biblical principles that will empower you to cross over into a whole new world of the courageous leadership role HE intends you to walk in.

My big thoroughbred is named Pax because I find peace when I am on his back... Ronald Reagan once said, "The best thing for the inside of a man is the back side of a horse!" AMEN! I find a connection to my Creator riding HIS majestic creations. In this picture Pax is cantering sideways at a 45 degree angle... he is most responsive and very impressive.

Chapter One — Submission to Master Demonstration

(Many of these photo's are still shots taken from video which causes them to be somewhat blurred.)

The horse you see running freely here in this round pen is what I want you to focus on. This demonstration is not about me or my ability to train horses. This is about seeing GOD's principles of Dominion and Submission and to see fear and courage in action.

God gave man (in Adam) dominion over every living creature... we just don't exercise that dominion. Today we, this mighty steed and I, are going to show you fear, rebellion, defiance, submission and finally courage as this horse makes the choice to step across the line.

Horses are like small children, very curious, but for as big and majestic as they are they are very fearful animals. The intention of what I am about to do, is to do to this horse what GOD does to us... remind it of my presence until the time comes when it will realize I am master and step across that line from rebellion to submission.

Right now as full of itself as this horse appears, its actions are motivated by fear. But just like us it will become complacent in its fear and begin to act out rebellion to mask that fear.

I am going to use a lunge whip... not to hit the horse but to keep its attention... it won't take the horse long to overcome it's initial fear of me... it will become secondary to it's curiosity of what I want. Horses have two basic defenses, "Flight or fight"... they prefer flight and will continue to run from me as it tries to understand what's going on.

As you can see this horse out weighs me, it can out run me and is most assuredly stronger than I. Having said all that, as majestic as this animal is in its present mindset it is totally useless. Just like us, all it is doing is taking up space... it has no purpose or direction.

As I continue to remind this horse that I am here, watch it's mindset change... it will begin just trying to get away... it will soon determine that it is not possible and will try to figure out how to take control. Once it understands I am not going away or giving in... it will go into a mindset of rebellion... it will try to change directions in defiance... trying to say, "You can make me run but I'll run in the direction I want!" You will see it flick its head, snort and generally act a fool. It will slowly decide that allowing me to be in charge is okay!

Once I see signs of submission begin I will drop the lunge whip and simply stand in the center of the round pen. If the horse is truly submissive it's time to begin building a trust relationship that will release the natural inborn courage GOD has placed in this animal. If the horse is truly at the point of submission it will turn and come directly to me. I then reward the good behavior with positive reinforcement, then turn and walk away... if the horse is truly ready to submit it will follow me as I walk away.

He now indicates submission... the operative word is "indicates."

This is the point where we are... when we turn to GOD because we are tired of the stress and struggles in life. It is time to see if this horse is ready to step across that line... is this true submission.

As GOD does with us, I will now explain my plan to the horse... just as GOD tells us in (Jeremiah 29:11), I will explain to the horse, I know the plan I have for this horse, it is for it's good not for it's harm, to give it a future and a hope. That's GOD's message to us and that's my message to this horse.

But this is when we discover the true motivation behind this submission attitude. I am now going to put a bit in its mouth and saddle on its back... as it says in the Epistle of James:

"Indeed we put bits in horse's mouths that they may obey us, and we turn their whole body." (James 3:33)

Once I introduce the bit and saddle, "the new rules", I will push the horse away to test it's motivation... a horse ready to submit will simply run around getting used to the bit in it's mouth and saddle on it's back and then turn back to me... but like us if the motivation was only to gain favor and not genuine submission we will see a rodeo of rebellion. This horse will explode bucking and running... trying to free itself of these "new rules."

That is the same thing we do with GOD... we submit with wrong motives and then rebel against the changes GOD requires.

Once our equine friend realizes it can't run from or buck off the "new rules"... it will then turn to me again and that's when the teaching process truly starts.

This horse will make mistakes along the way... none of them will be from evil intent... the mistakes will come because the horse doesn't understand what is required by its master. It has not listened to its master's voice long enough. But as this horse learns to listen it will grow and its trust in its master will release courage that will make it useful.

From this point on it is imperative that I NEVER, and I repeat, NEVER lose my temper with this majestic creature. As GOD does with us, ALL correction is done in LOVE, with a gentle hand and a soft word... be quick to listen, slow to speak and even slower to anger.

I must not do anything that would reintroduce fear into this animal's mindset. I must patiently work toward releasing the courage to trust me in everything... if this animal can grow to trust me, a mortal man, HOW MUCH MORE should we TRUST GOD.

As you are about to see... once a horse learns that it can trust its master it opens the door to unlimited potential... but five minutes of stupidity on my part will take a lifetime to overcome.

He has now decided to submit, but we saw that before. Now is the test of heart... is he really ready to join up and become useful.

The teaching starts here and will perfect itself through time.

Now I would like to introduce to you "Miss Leah" a 26 year old Champion cutting horse. As a 3 year old she won the National Futurity Cutting Horse Championship. "Leah" has been listening to her masters' voice for over a quarter century.

This mare is going to back up to the rail for me so this old grey haired cowboy can get on her bareback... saving me the embarrassment of trying to swing up on her back like I would have done in my youth.

Notice there is no saddle or bit... she is just submitting to her master because it is the desire of her heart...

Leah has been listening and learning her master's voice for so long that she even anticipates my desires... as I position myself she will begin to respond knowing what my every movement means.

Leah patiently awaits her saddle and bit... she is not tied or restrained in any way or fashion. She could simply walk away... but she wants to come together and accomplish something.

Leah willingly accepts the bit and eagerly awaits her chance to demonstrate her submission… it's as though she knows GOD is using her to touch lives.

With an instantaneous response to my leg pressure and the reins on her neck she moves to the right and to the left at my command.

She spins; she backs… she runs backwards and slides to a stop.

She goes from a standing stop to a dead run in flash... weaving and turning... backing and stopping at my every command. She loves being a part of something useful... she loves having meaning to her life.

And then just as quickly as we began, she goes right back to calm and peaceful... waiting for her master to ask of her again.

Now I am not standing on "Leah's" back to show off... I'm doing it to demonstrate how much this mare trusts me. The fact is this beautiful mare is showing you what GOD requires of you... it's called BLIND TRUST!

This wonderfully submissive mare that you just witnessed doing all of this is totally blind... she can't see a thing. She has no idea what's in front of her... yet because I ask she will go from standing to running without question.

Left in a pasture "Leah" barely moved around at all...she couldn't see and was afraid... but the minute she heard my voice she became courageous... she knew I would not lead her into danger... even if she were to walk through the valley of the shadow of death... with me riding her she would fear no evil. She responded with the courage of BLIND TRUST. Imagine how different your life would be if you would TRUST GOD BLINDLY.

Our precious friend and noble mount went home to be with the LORD at sundown, February 18, 2009... she will be sorely missed but never forgotten. And through this book and our DVD, she will continue to touch lives. Thank You LORD allowing me to be taught by this wonderful mare... I am truly a blest man.

Chapter Two — Overcoming Fear / Understanding Courage

Before you go any further... go to the LORD in prayer... ask HIM to open your eyes and heart, and then ask yourselves these questions:

What do you see in this demonstration that reminded you of yourself?

What do you think GOD is saying to you today through these majestic creatures?

How will the principles you just witnessed change you?

How can you apply these principles to your walk with GOD?

Well it's now time to get down to business... if I were to sit down with each of you, one on one, face to face... if we were to open our hearts to one another... I believe each of you would say that you would be willing to do whatever it took to be the man GOD wants you to be, the husband your wife deserves and the father your children can be proud of. But that will take a courage that only comes from GOD. That will take a willingness to let the old man die and learn to trust and obey your GOD and FATHER. That is a whole new world across the line... it requires you to take that step… but before you make that commitment I want to share a word GOD gave me in July of 2006.

"You can not let mood swings challenge GOD's word to you. Grow up into your salvation, so that bold confidence in GOD will characterize your daily life.

When you read Psalms 23, remember the words, 'I will fear NO EVIL'… aren't words of a nursery rhyme, they are HIS WORDS to help you live by HIS GRACE regardless of how ominous things seem.

If you seek GOD, HE will answer you, HE will deliver you from ALL your fears. Not only will GOD protect you from danger, He will also rescue you from those nagging fears of the 'what ifs and what might have beens'. That kind of anxiety creates spiritual chaos, robbing you of GOD's joy and GOD's peace.

Having faith doesn't mean you can't be honest with HIM about your struggles with fear. Everyone has areas of structural weakness even David who found special favor with GOD. It led him to write:

"When I am afraid I will trust in you…
In GOD whose words I praise,
In GOD I trust I will NOT BE AFRAID…
What can mortal man do to me?"

You will be assaulted by fears of every kind. DO NOT

let them find a resting place in your heart. Stand in confidence and GOD will dethrone your fear and keep it from ruling your life. Walk in faith, NOT by sight. DO NOT BE AFRAID, JUST BELIEVE!

GOD is at work in you and how long it takes is predicated on how much resistance there is… HE desires to fill your heart and mind with unspeakable joy… there is NO ROOM for fear! HE wants to cleanse your heart of ALL FEAR that you might exude HIS presence to ALL that you encounter, get out of HIS way and let GOD complete the work which HE has begun.

When GOD created man (in Adam), they fellowshipped daily and he had a presence that exuded GOD's peace and joy which he lost when he sinned against GOD.

Jesus, your LORD and SAVIOR walked the earth as a man for thirty years… and when the HOLY SPIRIT descended upon HIM… that same joy and peace began to exude from HIM to all HE encountered. It gave confidence to those seeking to believe. People today need to see real integrity in a man that is consistent with the HOLY SPIRIT. That Spirit that indwells you in the same Spirit that descended on JESUS.

You have been 'Chosen' to give confidence to others… to lift their spirits towards GOD. Allow HIS SPIRIT to shine through you… be the light HE has ordained you to be. PUT DOWN ALL FEAR AND DOUBT… TRUST AND OBEY!"

I believe with all my heart that the overall effectiveness of all men today is dependent upon the internalization of an Authentic Masculine relationship with GOD. This can only be accomplished by intimate, passionate FELLOWSHIP with HIM.

My grandfather told me years ago…

"Show me a man who knows the Word of God… and I will show you a man who can talk the talk.

But you show me a man who knows the GOD of the WORD and I'll show you a man who WALKS the WALK!"

Child of GOD, let's go meet the GOD of the WORD face to face…

LET'S STEP ACROSS THE LINE!

Join me in this prayer…

Father, we know YOU are already in our midst…but our prayer TODAY… as we come together in agreement… NOT just with each other… but with YOUR WORD… our prayer LORD GOD is that YOU manifest YOURSELF to us in a way that overwhelms each and everyone of us… bring us to our knees… change our hearts LORD… open our eyes and ears to YOUR precious HOLY SPIRIT IN JESUS NAME… AMEN!

I want to once again invite you to step across the line from believer to knower. But by the expression on your faces I can tell I need to explain what I mean.

Let's suppose that you have been raised in an

environment that was all electric… no one you know smokes… you have never experienced FIRE. You are invited to a campout… the campfire is blazing and you are about to enjoy your first ever "roasted marshmallow". You place that white lump of sweetness on a stick and into the flames it goes. Just like those before you… the first try ends with your marshmallow falling off your stick and into the coals… not knowing better you decide to reach into the fire and retrieve your somewhat charred delicacy. Suddenly the man next to you grabs your hand and exclaims… NO! NO! NO! Fingers… meat… fire… heat… Bar-BQ… NO! NO! NO! He explains that he is a professional marshmallow roaster… he even shows you his gold watch from The National Brotherhood of Marshmallow Roasters, Teamster's Local 114… we're talking serious credentials… so you take him at this word and choose not to reach into the fire… you just became a believer!

As it happens, you are down to the last marshmallow… he says, "Never fear… I have a stash of marshmallows stored in a Tupperware container in the trunk of my car for just such an emergency!" He gives you the last marshmallow and off he goes… and as fate would have it you repeat your first mistake and off your marshmallow goes… right into the coals… you say to yourself… "SELF," he just doesn't understand how quick I really am… so in you reach… grabbing your treat and pulling it out… suddenly your hand sends an instant message to your brain... "There are 5 small but extremely painful bonfires clinging to your thumb and fingers... we could use a little help here..." You then find yourself dancing about slapping your hand on your chest and blowing on your finger tips in an attempt to put out the flames and ease the pain... you have just become a knower!

A believer is someone who has heard and accepted something as true... but a knower has stepped across the line... he has been touched by flames and has the scars to prove it!

Now the horse you watched this morning showed us the transition from fear, to trust, to courage... from doubting, to believing, to knowing... so let's spend sometime discovering where the fear we as men struggle with comes from and what affect it has had on the crisis of manhood in America.

To understand our crisis let's go back to the beginning...to the Garden of Eden. In Genesis 2:16-17 we read....

"As the Lord God commanded the man saying, 'of every tree of the Garden you may freely eat, but of the tree of the knowledge of good and evil you shall NOT eat, for in the day that you eat of it you shall surely die'".

Who did GOD give the command to?

Where was the woman when GOD gave the command was given?

Let's read verses 20-25...

And the man gave names to all the cattle, and to birds of the sky, and to every beast of the field, but for Adam there was not found a helper suitable for him.

So the LORD God caused a deep sleep to fall upon the man, and he slept; then He took one of his ribs, and closed up the flesh at that place.

And the LORD God fashioned into a woman the rib which He had taken from the man, and brought her to the man...

And the man said,
"This is now bone of my bones,
And flesh of my flesh;
She shall be called Woman,
Because she was taken out of Man."

For this cause a man shall leave his father and his mother, and shall cleave to his wife; and they shall become one flesh. And the man and his wife were both naked and were not ashamed.

So we see the woman (Eve) had not yet been created... GOD never told Eve not to eat of the tree. It was Adam's place to explain the rules to his helpmate and to establish his position as head of his family. Obviously he failed.

Now let's read Chapter 3 verses 1-7 and see how the story unfolds.

Now the serpent was craftier than any beast of the

field, which the LORD God has made. And he said to the woman, "Indeed, has God said, 'You shall not eat from any tree of the garden'?"

And the woman said to the serpent, "From the fruit of the trees of the garden we may eat; but from the fruit of the tree which is in the middle of the garden, God has said, 'You shall not eat from it or touch it, lest you die.'"

And the serpent said to the woman, "You surely shall not die! "For God knows that in the day you eat from it your eyes will be opened, and you will be like God, knowing good and evil."

When the woman saw that the tree was good for food, and that it was a delight to the eyes, and that the tree was desirable to make one wise, she took from its fruit and ate; and she gave also to her husband with her, and he ate

Then the eyes of both of them were opened, and they knew that they were naked; and they sewed fig leaves together and made themselves loin coverings.

- What do you think the serpent looked like?
- When the serpent deceived Eve where was Adam?
- What effect did eating the fruit have on Eve?
- What effect did eating the fruit by Adam cause?
- Who was Eve disobedient to?
- Who was Adam disobedient to?

Now let's read verses 8-17…

And they heard the sound of the LORD God walking in the garden in the cool of the day, and the man and his wife hid themselves from the presence of the LORD God among the trees of the garden.

Then the LORD God called to the man, and said to him, "Where are you?"

And he said, "I heard the sound of Thee in the garden, and I was afraid because I was naked; so I hid myself."

And He said, "Who told you that you were naked? Have you eaten from the tree of which I commanded you not to eat?"

And the man said, "The woman whom Thou gavest to be with me, she gave me from the tree, and I ate."

Then the LORD God said to the woman, "What is this you have done?" And the woman said, "The serpent deceived me, and I ate."

And the LORD God said to the serpent, "Because you have done this, cursed are you more than all cattle, and more than every beast of the field; on your belly shall you go, and dust shall you eat all the days of your life; And I will put enmity between your seed and her seed; he shall bruise you on the head, and you shall bruise him on the heel."

To the woman He said, "I will greatly multiply your pain in childbirth, in pain you shall bring forth children; yet your desire shall be for your husband, and he shall rule over you."

Then to Adam He said, "Because you have listened to the voice of your wife, and have eaten from the tree about which I commanded you, saying, 'You shall not eat from it'; cursed is the ground because of you; in toil you shall eat of it all the days of your life.

What were Adam's first three responses following his disobedience? What did all three have in common?

What was his verbal response when GOD asked him if he ate of the tree?

Who all did he blame?

When GOD asked Eve what she had done, how did she respond?

How should have Adam responded?

Now let's read Ephesians 5:25-30...

Husbands, love your wives, just as Christ also loved the church and gave Himself up for her; that He might sanctify her, having cleansed her by the washing of water with the word, that He might present to Himself the church in all her glory, having no spot or wrinkle or any such thing; but that she should be holy and blameless.

So husbands ought also to love their own wives as their own bodies. He who loves his own wife loves himself, for no one ever hated his own flesh, but nourished and cherished it, just as Christ also does the church, because we are members of His body.

When men (in Adam) were removed from the Garden of Eden, the loss was immeasurable. Adam's disobedience cost men their relationship with GOD, their relationship with woman, and every form of purposeful, authentic life. The abundant and eternal life of the kingdom of Heaven was exchanged for an empty, tiresome, conflict filled and hopeless existence in a world of broken men. As a result, men suffered from a loss of authentic value, identity and function. Battered by the forces of darkness and evil, men are failing to lead in their homes, churches, and communities.

Faced with a barrage of lies integrated into a world system designed by Satan, men feel powerless to overcome the grip of sin living in the members of their body. They also feel hopeless in a quest of overcoming a sea of people operating in lies and confusion. Trapped in a web of deception, men have adopted pitiful and destructive models of manhood and male headship.

All the statistical evidence, substance abuse, crime, health problems, suicide, education, and mental health, supports the conclusion that men have been losing the battle against the flesh, the world and the forces of evil. This trend must be reversed through the authentic chain of authority that GOD has established. Therefore, in order to restore relationships in the Body of Christ, move forward the great commission, and provide a culture in which people can grow in sanctification and Holiness, something must be done to build spiritual growth of men.

The State of Manhood in America

(Statistical evidence)

Substance Abuse: Six times more men are arrested for drug abuse than women. For every woman arrested for drunkenness, more than ten men will be arrested for drunkenness and incarcerated. Over 88% of all drunk drivers are men. (This tells us men are lonely, fearful, and desperate).

Crime: 81% of all arrests are male arrests. 90% of all arrests for serious crimes are male arrests. FBI statistics reflect that a person is over 61/2 times more likely to be murdered by a man than by a woman. 7 out of 8 arsonists are men. Men are 25 times more likely to end up in prison. 79% of property crime offenders are male. In juvenile crime, the arrest rate for boys is 365% higher than for girls.

Health: Men live an average of seven years less than women. Men suffer far more from ulcers and other stress-related diseases than do their female counterparts. Men are more likely to die from cancer, pneumonia, liver disease, strokes, hardening of the arteries, and heart failure (deceived into choosing a life of stress that is killing us). Suicide: 75% of suicides are male. (Men are giving up, no hope left)

Education and Mental Health: Boys outnumber girls 3 to 1 in mental institutions. More than 66% of students who fail one or more grades are boys. Learning and behavioral disorders are 3 to 10 times more common among young males as among females of the same age. Among students who stutter, boys outnumber girls roughly 4 to 1. The vast majority of school dropouts are boys. (Something is wrong in the system... wrong for boys).

Academic World: The academic world reflects a vacuum, as illustrated by the curricula offered to the 100,000 undergraduates of the University of California. (Home of modem educational thinking), 4 of their 9 campuses offer BA degrees in Women's Studies, no corresponding degrees are offered in Men's Studies. The university intercampus library computer listings show the following: 762 items under the heading of "men" 14,289 items under the heading of "women" (1,800% more information about women than men) "The great outpouring of words about the contemporary American woman these past few years have made it seem as though the male either had no problems or didn't count enough to have them aired."

But Child of GOD, that is just part of the problem. The decline in Godly male leadership, resulting in men who lack the desire to stay committed through thick and thin, is destroying the family. In the United States, from 1960 to 2007, the number of children living with a divorced parent increased 394%... that percentage would be higher but for the fact that fewer people having children are even bothering to get married in the first place.

And this is what results from children living in

fatherless homes:

- 52 times more likely to commit suicide.
- 32 times more likely to run away.
- 20 times more likely to have behavioral disorders.
- 14 times more likely to commit rape.
- 9 times more likely to drop out of school.
- 10 times more likely to abuse chemical substances.
- 20 times more likely to end up in prison.
- 9 times more likely to end up in a state operated institution.

Fifty-percent of all children witness the breakup of their parent's marriage. More than half of those children will see the breakup of their parent's second and third marriages.

Divorced adults quadrupled from 4.3 million in 1970 to 18.9 million today... but the most alarming part of that figure is the realization that the divorce rate among those professing to be Christians is higher than non-Christians. That should not be so.

A survey that speaks volumes to my point reveals that in rating life goals those Christians surveyed... #6 was "desiring to have a close personal relationship with GOD." #2 was "living a comfortable lifestyle"... and #1 was "Being happy!" How sad.

In recent years there has emerged a vast array of "men's movements" to counter this trend... I have watched, studied and attended many of them. My conclusion, based on the lack of results I have witnessed is that too much of what is being offered is nothing more than elaborate "PEP RALLIES" with an abundance of emotional flash and little to no substantive change.

The problem with most of these movements is they look inward. They seek to resolve the spiritual crisis of the American male, a group by the way that paradoxically dominates the American Prison population as overwhelmingly as it does the U.S. Senate. This crisis cannot be resolved inwardly, by what GOD calls relying on our own understanding... it can only be resolved vertically, by trusting HIM. We MUST submit to the Authentic role GOD has ordained for men... and that requires stepping across the line from fear to courage.

We first need to lift the confusion of what Biblical masculine courage is all about. What I am about to submit for our consideration would not fall into the category of "Politically Correct" but since it is "Scripturally Correct" I boldly state that Courage is a masculine distinctive and the exercise of courage is an authentic masculine function.

The secular world tells us that Webster's defines courage as "Strength of mind and spirit that enables one to control fear when facing danger; bravery". And The American College Dictionary defines it as, "The quality of mind that enables one to encounter difficulties and danger with firmness or without fear; bravery. To act consistently with ones opinion".

But GOD's word tells us that courage is, "a man choosing to sacrifice the temporal for the eternal, facing his fear and choosing obedience".

We live in a time when we have no true heroes anymore, there is a vacuum of leadership and there is NO ONE in a position of visibility and leadership to admire! We live in a day dominated by opinion polls and situation ethics.

Cynicism continues to grow in America because courage, a very singular characteristic of leadership, is practically invisible today, is it possible that we live in a land filled with fear, or is it more accurate to say a land filled with cowards?

Webster says a coward is, "one who shows disgraceful fear or timidity". To be cowed is "to be intimidated with threats or show of strength". To be cowardly "implies a weak or ignoble lack of courage". Even reading these words should stir uncomfortable emotions for many men.

Most men I know prefer not to even hear the word coward. After all, our culture says to be afraid is not manly.

However, in spite of the cultural prohibition men are afraid because fear runs rampant in our society. Intuitively men know they are not adequate, that they don't measure up. As a result, they are constantly fighting feelings of insecurity and hiding their sense of inadequacy. There must be a better way to live and there is.

Man was designed from the beginning to exercise courage... GOD designed men for leadership (authentic headship and authority) and courage is foundational to leadership. GOD also gave man the ability to choose obedience. Today, the man who knows Christ, and has the indwelling of the HOLY SPIRIT, has the privilege, responsibility and potential power to exercise courage. Courage is a masculine distinction and an authentic masculine function.

How can we know GOD designed men for the exercise of courage? Because every time the word appears in the Scripture it is in a masculine context. Throughout the scripture only men are exhorted to be courageous. I would be remiss if I did not say that women down through history have demonstrated extraordinary courage... this is not a contest... but GOD designed man to exercise courageous leadership. One of the earliest occasions is when Moses is exhorting Joshua to be "strong and courageous". The LORD exhorts Joshua three times in the same address "to be strong and courageous". After Joshua had issued commands to the officers of the people (men) they answered him with their commitment of obedience and they exhorted their own commander to "only be strong and courageous!"

We find David exhorting his son Solomon to be

courageous. Asa is finding courage to take down "the abominable idols" and "restore the alter of the LORD". Jehoshaphat charged "some of the Levites and some of the Priest, and some of the heads of the fathers households of Israel (men) to act with courage". Hezekiah exhorted his military officers to be "strong and courageous".

In the New Testament JESUS said to HIS (male) disciples, "Take courage". Paul told the men with whom he was ship wrecked "to keep up your courage". He said to Corinthian men "be men of courage; be strong". There is also the testimony of the enemies of Christ... "When they saw the courage of Peter and John and realized that they were unschooled, ordinary men, they were astonished and they took note that these men had been with JESUS."

I again remind you Scripture tells us of courageous women... Ruth, Esther, and Deborah for example. But if you look closely... you will find that these women were all faced with their situations because of earlier cowardice and failure of one or more men. Obviously women have exercised courage throughout the centuries, but this is not a distinctive of the female design. Courage is a masculine design. If there is NO courage in the land, then men are responsible for the vacuum.

Masculine courage has liberating power. Wherever authentic masculine courage is exercised, a climate of freedom and liberation is created. Others are encouraged;

their courage is restored and sustained as long as men continue their GOD ordained privilege.

An obvious illustration is found in the life of David, when he encountered the Philistine giant, Goliath. (1st Samuel 17) According to Scripture, the men of Israel had retreated from the Giant "and were greatly afraid".

When David confronted the giant he said, "... you come to me with a sword, a spear, a javelin, but I come to you in the NAME of the LORD of Hosts, the GOD of the Armies of Israel, whom you have taunted. This day the LORD will deliver you into my hands..." And the rest is history...to fully understand David's courage look at what seems insignificant in this Scripture... but speaks volumes to this young shepherd's courage... in 1st Samuel 17:40 we see that "Little David" "chose for himself five smooth stones from the brook..." Why five? Well it seems that Goliath had 4 grown sons... David went prepared to whip the whole family (2 Sam. 21:22). He knew stepping across the line between fear and courage would involve risks... he stepped out prepared.

The Bible is replete with masculine courage... the liberating power of masculine courage is evident when David acted with courage, the men of Israel and Judah were liberated from fear. They were encouraged, their courage was restored and the enemies of the kingdom were terrified and fled.

Some years ago a black Pastor in the inner city of Chicago grew weary of preaching to his congregation on the evils of their community and seeing nothing done about it. So one Sunday he announced he was cutting this Sunday's sermon short... he was going outside the church to pray out loud for the drug dealers who regularly gathered right outside selling their wares. He invited all who would, to join him... only seven men chose to. As they prayed out loud they were ridiculed but continued to fervently pray. Soon the dealers became uncomfortable and began to drift away. Those men whose courage was empowered and set free by the HOLY SPIRIT led courage of their Pastor continue to take back block by block the Southside of the inner city of Chicago from area drug lords. But someone had to lead... Step across the line first... and GOD has delegated that responsibility and potential power to the man.

Men would like to be courageous, that is their preference. And some men seem to know this is their responsibility, to exercise this Authentic Masculine function. The problem is that men have been overly concerned with protecting themselves since the day they were born. Men are "Natural born" cowards. Fear has been defined as "the agitation or dismay in anticipation of or in the presence of danger" and for men, fear is the nemesis of courage and obedience.

The pattern was set for the male in the Garden of Eden. Adam's first three responses following his disobedience were responses of fear. He was first fearful and ashamed of his nakedness and hid behind fig leaves. His second response was to hide in the bushes when he remembered GOD would soon be looking for him to walk in the cool of the day. His third response was to hide behind the woman when confronted with his sin. He did not exercise courage when it came time to "face the music". He tried to "cover up" his fear with fig leaves and then like a frightened little boy he tried to run away and hide. Last and worst of all, he hid behind the "woman's skirt". Men have been covering up and hiding ever since.

Men especially fear that someone will discover that they are afraid. So they hide their inward sense of inadequacy, failure and cowardice. The truth is too painful to acknowledge.

So we are left with a world suffering from a vacuum of courage. But there are two ways to look at the problem of this vacuum. The first is the response of the man without Christ and the indwelling power of the HOLY SPIRIT. *(Expletives omitted!)*

"Well this is a fine kettle of fish! There is NO courage in the land and it's my fault, as if I'm not blamed for enough already!"

This man without Christ is not up to the task because the reality is, he is inadequate, and he cannot measure up. He will create great smoke screens to cover up his fears and to find "safe" places to hide. He will go to great lengths attempting to convince others of his adequacy, but ultimately he only deceives himself. JESUS said, "Apart from ME you can do nothing!" The man apart from Christ is destined to walk in the steps of a coward, never knowing authentic masculine courage.

The second response is the response of the man who knows Christ, walks with Christ, and is directed and empowered by the HOLY SPIRIT. His attitude is as follows,

"THANK YOU FATHER that YOU have designed me for the exercise of courage and have exhorted me to be strong and courageous. It has always been my experience that YOU never ask me to do anything that YOU do not empower me to do".

This man recognizes that he "can do all things through Christ who strengthens him". He counts on the fact that "HIS Grace is sufficient". This man declares "the LORD is my light and my salvation, whom then shall I fear". He has learned not to "fear those who kill the body, but are unable to kill the soul". He has experienced the restoration of his Spiritual heritage. He is a "knower".

It should be encouraging to know that the enemies of Christ are always afraid. It should also be encouraging to know that men who do not know Christ have "Hearts that melt within them," at the same moment Christ's love should stir our hearts with HIS compassion for those men who walk in fear and desperation.

And yet, I find that too many men who claim to know Christ continue to be controlled by the same basic terrors.

They experience the fear of not measuring up, the fear of failure, they fear losing control of the world around them and worst of all, they fear that someone will discover this truth about them. They are secretly asking themselves, "I wonder if other men are as uncertain as I am at this business of being a man... whatever this is anymore? I am moving through my life so quickly... my wife doesn't respect me and my kids are out of control. I hate this unsettled and insecure feeling. Men shouldn't feel this way."

So, how does the man who knows Christ deal with FEAR?

First don't deny the fear... honesty is the best policy... face it "Head on."

Fear is inherent in the flesh and unfortunately as long as we are on this earth we have to put up with our fallen flesh. The good news is the "old man," who had no alternative but to walk in fear is dead. We are "New Creatures in Christ," all that is left is the "power of indwelling sin," still resident in our flesh. But, we are "no longer subject" to our old fleshly responses because the flesh is no match for the Holy Spirit within us.

But, fear is a real emotion of the flesh and to deny it means we are being emotionally dishonest. In fact, to constantly deny that we experience fear becomes a form of fearing the emotion of fear itself. We cannot simply suppress it and pretend it doesn't exist. We must guard against taking the position that we will overcome it (in the flesh) even if it kills us... because it might do exactly that.

In one sense of the word, fear is only an emotion, but we are infinitely complex beings. GOD has intricately designed us. We use words to describe ourselves such as MIND, WILL and EMOTIONS or BODY, SOUL and SPIRIT. We would like to think we could separate ourselves into component parts, understanding those parts and deal with them individually. And, to the degree that in HIS wisdom it is necessary, we can. But, the final word is we are created in HIS image, and are in some measure transcendent beyond understanding. Our components are dynamic not static. Fear affects our minds, our wills, our emotions, our body, our soul but does not affect the HOLY SPIRIT who lives within us all.

It is imperative then, especially as men, that we be honest in the emotional dimensions of our lives as we are in the more cognitive dimensions. King David the "Man after GOD's heart" was perhaps the most emotionally honest man in Scripture. Like David in Psalm 51, we must acknowledge the truth about ourselves to our FATHER we must agree with what HE reveals and walk in freedom. Truthfully, we will never walk in freedom from the experience of fear. But, we CAN walk in freedom from its control.

In the Scriptures it is evident that GOD designed the man to face the most fearful threats of the enemy. In the

Garden of Eden, Satan went around the man to target the woman. After the fall, the man "was afraid." Now Satan's strategy is to use the fear in the man's heart to neutralize or "take out" the one designed for the exercise of courageous leadership. This strategy leaves the woman and the child vulnerable to greater attack.

For the male, an obedient choice will always require him to move through a wall of fear. A man must be prepared like an experienced long distance runner to "hit the wall" of exhaustion and still take that next step, anticipating new energy on the other side. Like the runner, the man who would be courageous must choose to hit the wall of fear and move through to a place of obedience and faith. It was courageous Joshua who made the obedient choice and said, "Choose this day whom you will serve, but as for me and my house we will serve the Lord."

Satan is the master deceiver and is an expert in manufacturing and magnifying consequences. The important principle to remember is no matter how great our fear, when we choose courageously, the outcome is never very severe as we have anticipated.

Beware of your natural tendency as a man to SELL OUT your masculine potential for courage. The exercise of courage not only involves choices, but it always includes an understanding of risk.

In our culture, where do men choose to take risks?

What men top your list to admire?

Why?

The obvious answers are as we have seen... the world of economic enterprises, business, competitive sports, from football to mountain climbing, and of course the battlefield. These are all areas in which men take risks, because the world gives them palpable rewards they can see and feel. It provides momentary feelings of adequacy. That which is eternal and unseen is sacrificed for that which is temporal and has tangible evidence. Solomon, the wisest man who ever lived called it all "VANITY" and "Striving after the wind." Who would understand that better than Solomon?

A man deals with fear as he walks by faith. Walking by faith is the experience of the man who truly knows Christ!

"Those who know YOUR name will trust in YOU, for YOU LORD have never forsaken those who seek YOU," Psalm 9:10

Faith defeats fear...but fear must be dealt with to effectively walk in faith. Walking by faith is the experience of the man who truly "KNOWS CHRIST!" Again... faith defeats fear. A man can only face the threat of danger with courage given by the HOLY SPIRIT. "It is not by might nor by power, but by my Spirit, says the LORD ALMIGHTY." Spirit powered authentic masculine courage moves a man through his wall of fear to faith. Courage is the leading edge of faith in a man's life.

Walking by faith will always involve choices and the quality of the man's courage is demonstrated by the choices he makes. Real courage and real faith will always make obedient choices. It is the way of a coward to yield to fear and choose disobedience. Living by faith becomes a life long series of exciting opportunities to trust and obey.

Personally, I have never found a decision of my flesh to pay any dividends other than anxiety, unhappiness, discouragement, failure, guilt, pain, despair, frustration and aimlessness. On the other hand, I have never found the courageous choice of obedience to pay any dividends other than peace, confidence, satisfaction, purpose, certainty, freedom, joy, hope, and love.

When you honestly compare the alternatives, there is no contest. The bondage of fear is the consequence and constant companion of the man who walks in disobedience. The man who chooses disobedience has chosen to walk in the steps of a coward and live a meaningless life. He must constantly prop himself up with lies. He may deceive himself and occasionally those closest to him, but the tension of maintaining this "house of straw" is a life of fear and misery. For the man who would exercise courage and obey GOD there is freedom and power and joy in the HOLY SPIRIT.

Gradually, as you obediently walk in power of the HOLY SPIRIT and stand on the promises of HIS word the walls of fear in your life will begin to crumble. You will increasingly experience the faithfulness of HIS "unfailing love." The determining factor will always be whose power do you walk in. Are you willing to "Step across the line?"

The unfortunate truth today is that too many men who profess to be Christians are held captive by a sense of inadequacy, uncertainty, and fear! The one who is here to steal, kill and destroy has robbed most men of their GOD ordained masculinity. They live Spiritually impotent lives. Tragically, a vast reservoir of potential Spiritual leadership and courage remains behind a dam, a dam constructed by the enemy. The great irony is that the dam is merely a dam of deception.

Personally, I am convinced no man who follows Christ would choose to remain in such condition if he were provided an authentic alternative.

As the Apostle Paul encouraged..." we must walk in the Spirit... we must heed the words of the Apostle Peter..." and diligently add to your faith, virtue, to your virtue knowledge, to knowledge self-control, to self-control perseverance, to perseverance godliness, to godliness brotherly kindness, and to brotherly kindness LOVE."

We must faithfully do everything according to the Scriptures and pray for a breakthrough. I believe the only way to achieve that breakthrough is to get on our knees and cry out to GOD and together we shall see the destruction of the dam. Then our land will be flooded with men of great courage and faith, men who lead by the power of Christ's love and the sacrifice of their own lives... I believe, this fundamental crisis, unless resolved, will continue to destroy men individually, their families and eventually the culture they represent. Men, our women have had enough, they are tired of putting up with childish, selfish, cowardly men. Little boys who have never grown up!

These are questions we need to answer before we proceed:

What area or areas of your life do you see as the biggest obstacle between you now and the one GOD desires?

Why do some men grow more rapidly than others?

A gray-haired cowboy Preacher once said,

"The man who knows how will always have a job... BUT the man who knows why will sign his paycheck!"

So how do we move from knowing how, to knowing why?

God's word says, "Seek and you shall find..." but that requires courage... because seeking may reveal or expose things about ourselves that we don't like or more to the point, we don't want to know.

Masculine courage is an authentic, intricate part of God's design for man. JESUS Himself gave us, by HIS example the characteristic that is essential to masculine courage: PEACE. It is a peace that defies human understanding and therefore cannot be achieved in the flesh.

When it came time for JESUS to begin HIS ministry the HOLY SPIRIT descended on HIM and with that anointing came that very PEACE. The Peace that defies all human understanding. JESUS then went about selecting twelve men to follow HIM and learn from HIM for the next three years. GOD chose each of HIS disciples because each had something in their heart that would minister to us today.

These twelve men marveled at the peace they witnessed in JESUS those three years. Their Master was never afraid. HE was always calm, never stressed or ruffled by any circumstance.

We know Christ was capable of Spiritual anger. At times HE was stirred, and HE knew how to weep. But HE led HIS life on earth as a man at peace... NOT a man of peace... a man at peace.... at total peace. HE had peace with HIS Father, peace in the face of temptation, peace in the face of rejection and mockery. He even had peace during storms at sea; sleeping while others trembled with terror.

HIS disciples had witnessed HIM being dragged to a high ridge by an angry mob determined to kill HIM. Yet HE calmly walked away from that scene, untouched and full of peace. They had heard men call their LORD a devil. Religious leaders pointed to HIM as a fraud. Some groups plotted to kill HIM. Yet, through it all JESUS never lost HIS peace. NO man, NO religious system, NO devil could rob HIM of HIS peace.

I can imagine all this caused discussion among the disciples:

"How could HE sleep in a storm? What kind of peace is that? How could HE be so calm when the crowd was about to throw HIM over a cliff? People mock HIM, insult HIM, and spit on HIM, but always HE stays at peace. NOTHING disturbs HIM."

JESUS said,

"Peace I leave with you, My peace I give you; not as the world gives do I give to you. Let not your heart be troubled, neither let it be afraid." (John 14:27)

This wasn't going to be the so-called peace of a numb, zoned-out society. Nor would it be the temporary peace of the rich and famous, who try to purchase peace of mind with material things. It wasn't going to be the false peace of those deceived into thinking through the stubbornness of their own minds they can have peace.

No this was the very PEACE of Christ Himself, a peace that surpasses all human understanding.

JESUS attempted to prepare them for what was about to happen... but their limited finite minds were unable to comprehend. HE told them HE was about to be killed.... That, "The HOLY SPIRIT would guide them through what they were about to face. HE would be their friend. The HOLY SPIRIT would enable them to experience this peace JESUS would give them."

Yet these men had no concept of who the HOLY

SPIRIT was! They simply wouldn't understand the promise of the HOLY SPIRIT until the day of Pentecost!

We who have accepted Christ have the indwelling of the HOLY SPIRIT and have the ability to walk in HIS peace... That peace JESUS has given us. But the "Father of lies" has us deceived... he would have us believe we aren't worthy of living in Christ's peace... that we have too many struggles in our life. And we acquiesce because our faith is weak.

We can learn much by considering those twelve men who JESUS first gave HIS peace. None were worthy, none had a right to it... and all were weak in faith.

Think about Peter. JESUS was about to bestow HIS peace on a minister of the gospel who soon would be spewing denials and cursing. Peter may have been zealous in his love for Christ, but he was about to deny HIM.

Then there was James and John, men with a competitive spirit, always seeking to be recognized. They asked to sit on JESUS right and left hand when HE ascended to HIS throne in glory.

Yet the other disciples were no more righteous. They simmered with anger toward James and John for trying to upstage them. There was Thomas, a man given to doubt. All of the disciples were so lacking in faith it amazed and distressed JESUS. Indeed, in Christ's most troubling hour, they would all forsake HIM and flee. Even after the Resurrection, when the word spread that "JESUS is

Risen..." The disciples were "slow to believe." And when the LORD appeared to them HE chastised them for their lack of faith.

But there's even more. These were also confused men. They didn't understand the ways of the LORD, HIS parables confused them, after the crucifixion, they lost all sense of unity and authentic purpose they once had, scattering in all directions.

What a mirrored reflection these men are of us... full of fear, unbelief, disunity, sorrow, confusion, competitiveness, and pride. Yet it was to these same troubled servants that JESUS said, "I am going to give you My Peace!"

Why was this promise of supernatural peace given to such flawed men? Why was it given to us? Because they, like us, have been called and chosen in CHRIST and for NO OTHER REASON. They weren't chosen because they were good or righteous or talented or had ability. NOR WERE WE!

All men are called by GOD to be empowered by the HOLY SPIRIT to experience the peace that comes through authentic masculine courage. But only a remnant few will have the commitment of heart to achieve it!

Show me a man who is committed to be more like Christ... whose heart is set on trusting the HOLY SPIRIT to remove all stumbling blocks.... And I will show you a man whom Satan cannot defeat. The Peace of CHRIST flows to all who are determined to trust the HOLY

SPIRIT to shape them into JESUS' likeness.

We must do as HIS disciples did after Pentecost... they became strong and courageous, walking in the Spirit recognizing "the old man is dead!" They went from believer to knower.

We must break the dam of discouragement that holds the men of the church today in bondage. I hear it all the time from Christian men... men in the church..." yes I believe in GOD... I know HE loves me... but right now that all seems like empty theology... I don't need another sermon... I need a miracle!"

Well that miracle is waiting across that line... we are about to find clarity of purpose as we learn the "key" to experiencing authentic masculine courage.

Chapter Three — Finally The Key

Before I introduce you to the "KEY" to finally experiencing the joy of walking in Authentic Masculine Courage, we must first grasp some critical essentials to sustaining that courageous life.

There are three essentials for sustaining courage in the life of a man. This is first assuming the man understands his utter dependence upon the HOLY SPIRIT, and that he understands how to draw upon the Power of the Spirit to live by faith.

First, the man must have unshakable confidence in GOD's intrinsic goodness. If we do not believe GOD is good, then there is no foundation for our courage. Further, this confidence must be based upon our experience with GOD versus our information about GOD.

An example of information-based "confidence" in GOD has been demonstrated to us by King Saul. His knowledge of GOD was second hand experience... "I heard that I heard that I heard," instead of "I know that I know that I know..." Whatever Saul knew about GOD and HIS nature was limited to what he heard from Samuel who had a substantial base of experience with

GOD. Saul's personal experience base with the goodness of GOD was slight at best.

On the other hand David had first hand knowledge of GOD... his was experience-based confidence, as was Joshua's, which we will see in a moment. I believe GOD acknowledged David as a "man after GOD's heart" because David truly understood the goodness and love of GOD better than any human who has ever lived. David understood and counted upon the very essence of God's nature, HIS love. That is why we learn more about GOD's attributes from David than anyone in Scripture, and the apparent freedom David experienced with GOD is unparalleled. I believe David understood his own depravity and was more honest about it than anyone else as well.

David's experience with God's goodness began early with a lion and a bear. This base of experience with GOD sustained David's courage when he met Goliath on the field of Battle, as we discussed before.

Joshua also had an experience-based confidence with GOD's goodness. He personally witnessed the miracles of Moses, the night of Passover, deliverance from Pharaoh, crossing the Red Sea, the provision of Manna, quail and water from the rock for the children of Israel in the wilderness, and the defeat of their enemies. Joshua's experience is acknowledged by GOD as HE refers to HIMSELF nine times in the eight verses of HIS charge to Joshua to lead the people into the Promised Land.

If our confidence in GOD's goodness is based only upon Biblical "information" we will fail and prove ourselves cowards. We must KNOW HIS goodness in terms of our own personal experience with HIM.

Second, courage is sustained in a man's life by "meditating upon the word of GOD night and day." GOD was very clear to Joshua when HE said,

"Be strong and courageous. Be careful to obey all the law my servant Moses gave you; do not turn from it to the right or to the left, that you may be successful wherever you go. Do not let this book of the law depart from your mouth; meditate on it day and night, so that you may be careful to DO everything written in it. Then you will be prosperous and successful."

What happens if men designed and instructed to provide courageous leadership, fail to see GOD's direction and follow HIS word? When a man takes things into his own hands and depends on his own wisdom, he is ALWAYS deceived. Consequences follow for the men who were deceived and for those whom they are responsible.

Without the ongoing, continual counsel of GOD's word, sharper than any two edged sword, dividing that which is true from that which is false, men fall into snares. When men are caught in snares their fear increases and they become further ensnared. Without confidence and certainty of GOD's goodness, men walk in fear. Cowardice becomes their experience!

The THIRD way courage is sustained in a man's life is through authentic, masculine fellowship. Unfortunately most men learn to become islands unto themselves from their childhood. The tendency is to see another man as a potential competitor or threat. Authentic, masculine fellowship has two essential dimensions. The first dimension has to do with relationships that are accountable unto death. The men of Joshua reflected this commitment in their relationships. They said,

"Whatever you have commanded us we will do, and wherever you send us we will go. Just as we fully obeyed Moses, so we will obey you. Only may the Lord your GOD be with you as HE was with Moses. Whoever rebels against your word and does not obey your words, whatever you command them, will be put to death. Only be strong and courageous."

Their commitment to one another was great; it was all on the line. (Joshua 1:16-18).

Today what is needed is the death of masculine flesh. It is true that woman completes the man, but she is not fully adequate for his development. Most men find it difficult for their flesh to "die" in the presence of a woman. They don't think and feel the way we do. It takes other men. James wrote, "Therefore confess your sins to each other and pray for each other so that you may be healed." This is a command and it is solely directed to the MAN. Once again Scripture needs to be read and interpreted from a masculine perspective. Trust, freedom, honesty, like-mindedness, accountability and commitment make up the environment of authentic, masculine fellowship.

These relationships that are accountable unto death of our flesh, also include emotional honesty. In our culture the only time it is socially acceptable for a man to be emotionally honest is when he is drunk, or when he is facing death in a foxhole. A Biblical model of emotional honesty is illustrated in the relationship between David and Jonathan (1 Sam.18:1) "The soul of Jonathan was knit to the soul of David," It is also interesting that each of them were men of courage and men whose confidence was in GOD. They were easily "kindred spirits."

The Second dimension of authentic, masculine fellowship is the battle. The men who marched into the Promised Land with Joshua represented the only generation of Old Testament men who were faithful until they were "gathered to their Fathers." The most significant factor in their faithfulness was the Battle. They remained on the field of battle the majority of their lives. Their lives reflected infinite purpose... they knew the "thrill of battle." (Joshua 1:1-9)

Today the battle is for the hearts and minds of men. JESUS called us to "make disciples of all the nations." (Matthew. 28:19-20). If a man is to find authentic masculine fellowship he will find it only in the context of battle.

GOD designed man to experience and exercise

authentic masculine courage… it is time to "trade up" for a new authentic experience of masculine freedom and power.

"Trading up" comes with a genuine filling of the HOLY SPIRIT in a man's life. The chief manifestations of that are the power and compelling nature of masculine love… the unique manifestation of CHRIST's love in a man… the power and definitive nature of masculine sacrifice… sacrifice that can change and define the man's world… and the liberating potential and power of masculine courage… a courage which initiates genuine faith and sustains freedom in a man's life and the lives of those around him.

As we noted earlier JESUS Himself is our greatest example of authentic masculine courage… but arguably CHRIST is a tough act to follow… many would cite that HE was GOD manifest in the flesh and we are but mortal men… so to make our quest seem more attainable let us consider one of the men Jesus hand picked to be His ambassador.

I submit to you "Saul of Tarsus" a.k.a., the Apostle Paul… who led by the Holy Spirit penned 13 of the 21 Epistles of the New Testament. And it is by studying the man Paul through his writings that GOD reveals the key to achieving Authentic Masculine Courage.

When we read Paul's Epistles we must read them in the order they were written to discover and understand how GOD worked in and through him to reveal the "key" to achieving Authentic Masculine Courage to us.

In his last Epistle, Paul exhorts Timothy to be a man of courage... "For GOD has not given us a spirit of TIMIDITY, but of power, and love and discipline." (The GREEK word translated "timidity" denotes a cowardly, shameful fear caused by a weak, selfish character. There's that word coward again).

When we chose to step across the line between our flesh and HIS HOLY SPIRIT, we will walk in the power of authentic masculine courage.

I was asked the question, "What does it mean to suffer for Christ's sake?" When the question was posed my Bible was open to Philippians. As I looked down verse 1:29 jumped off the page at me!

"For it has been granted for Christ sake, not only to believe in HIM, but also to suffer for His sake, experiencing the same conflict which you saw in me and now hear to be in me." (STILL) NASB.

We need to make note here of two critical points... I was about to respond with the traditional interpretation of this passage... "This refers to what the Philippians witnessed when Paul and Silas were imprisoned at Philippi (Acts 16:19-40)." (Sourced: The John MacArthur NASB Study Bible)

Notice Paul says the Philippians are experiencing the "same conflict" as he is.

They are not imprisoned so that would eliminate that interpretation.

Paul says this "conflict" is in him... that makes the conflict an inner struggle not an external one.

This little nugget of GOLD opened an understanding of the conflict that has changed my life forever. I immediately went to Romans 7:15... here Paul uses a mastery of words to convey a word picture of this *conflict*.

"For what I am doing, I do not understand; for I am not practicing what I would like to do, but I am doing the very thing I hate."

Then in verse 21 he writes:

"I find a principle that evil is present with me, the one who wants to do good."

Paul is acknowledging that there is a continual ongoing battle to overcome his flesh. It was not a fight between Paul and Satan... Paul was fighting himself. I went right back to Philippians 2:5.

"Have this attitude in yourselves which also was in Christ JESUS..."

The attitude that Paul is referring to is an attitude of obedience, an attitude only attainable by totally surrendering to the HOLY SPIRIT.

Once I grasped what the "Conflict" was... I found it necessary to research Paul's sojourn from trying to answer the call on his life relying on his own abilities in the flesh... to completely surrendering to the Holy Spirit.

I began by listing the Epistles of the New Testament by the date written. As I did I was reminded James'

Epistle was the first of all New Testament writings... circa AD 45. I purposed to read James right then and to my amazement found every word addressed how to walk victoriously through the "Conflict." But if James wrote these words 15 years before Paul figured it out... how did James know all this?

The answer is in knowing who James was. After Jesus was born Mary and Joseph had four sons, James, Joseph, Simon, and Jude... all half brothers to Jesus. Every word of the Epistle of James was imparted to him first hand by his "Big Brother" JESUS.

James became known as "James the Just" because of his intense devotion to righteousness... he had been groomed to walk victorious in a sinful world by JESUS Himself. Can you imagine the feeling of standing in front of the resurrected LORD of LORDS... KING of KINGS and realizing you had been mentored all your life by the promised Messiah! Talk about a life changing moment.

So, did Paul have access to the Epistle of James? You bet he did! Then why didn't Paul see what I see? My answer is simple... why did it take me 49 years of reading James to see it myself? It's actually not difficult to comprehend... but until you grasp what the "conflict" is... you cannot appreciate the depth of James' words. James puts it so simply:

"... *Submit to GOD. Resist the devil and he will flee...*"

To submit means "to line up under"... James uses this

word to describe a willing, conscious submission to GOD's authority as sovereign ruler of the universe. The flip side of this command to "submit" is to "resist" which literally means to take your stand against. All of us are either under the lordship of Christ or the lordship of Satan; there is no middle ground. Once we transfer our allegiance from Satan to GOD, Satan will flee... we have no battle with him... he is a defeated foe... our fight with him is over.

So when did Paul realize his fight was with himself?

Paul's first Epistle was Galatians followed by 1st and 2nd Thessalonians and then 1st Corinthians. Paul was being led through a process that would change him forever!

In 1st Corinthians 5:9 Paul refers to an Epistle he wrote to the church in Corinth before 1st Corinthians. Other than this reference we have no record of this letter or it's contents. Then sometime between 1st and 2nd Corinthians Paul wrote a seething letter to the Corinthians. In that letter Paul lost it... he allowed his temper and his pride to get the best of him and he told them off in no uncertain terms... In less than GODly terms. Paul makes mention of this letter and his regret in writing it starting in 2:3 of 2nd Corinthians.

Hebrew historian, Josephus, writes that Paul thought he had destroyed his ministry and disgraced GOD's calling on his life. He was depressed and thought his service to GOD was over.

Little did Paul know that it was all part of GOD's plan. GOD had orchestrated all of this to show Paul... and in doing so, show us... that no matter how intelligent you are... no matter how much you love GOD... if your efforts to serve HIM rely on flesh, you will fail miserably. GOD intended all of this to convey this profound Biblical truth to you and I. Jesus said... "A house divided against itself will not stand..." Flesh vs. flesh is a "NO WIN" proposition!

Paul had to be shown that attempting to overcome his flesh by the strength or reason of his own finite limited self was shear folly. Paul was chosen by GOD because HE knew Paul would try to fulfill his calling through his own skills... after all he was Paul. But once he grasped... "A house divided against itself will not stand..." he was changed forever.

With new clarity of purpose Paul wrote Romans, Ephesians and Philippians... and it was Philippians that opened my eyes to the reality that 1st John wasn't overly idealistic...it was absolutely attainable.

I suddenly realized that it was possible to live up to GOD's expectations of my life... and so can you. We can do as Paul, James, Peter, Jude and John exhorted. All we have to do is "enter in..." step across the line from the finite to the infinite... from the limited (our flesh) to the unlimited (the HOLY SPIRIT). The HOLY SPIRIT does not sin and cannot be tempted by sin. WOW! Can it be that easy...? YES IT IS! IT IS EXACTLY THAT EASY!

GOD has uniquely designed men to exhibit and exercise authentic masculine courage... we have been created by GOD to do battle... to be victorious over the enemy... and that enemy is us... the battle is within ourselves. We have been given the HOLY SPIRIT and the LORD says... "The battle is His..." Paul tells us what he learned first hand; we cannot win a Spiritual battle using the weapons of the flesh.

We must step out with boldness in the power of the HOLY SPIRIT and trust the results to GOD.

To step across the line we must be willing to die to self... but as men we have become masters at masking our true selves. Inside each of us is a scared little boy... a shamefully, frightened little boy who hides behind a façade we have been erecting for years. We must be willing to see ourselves for who we really are... men lacking authentic value, identity and function... men fighting a fleshly battle with cowardice and losing... running from moral and spiritual responsibility.

We must finally see ourselves *as Paul did....*

"When I was a child, I used to speak like a child, think like a child, reason like a child; when I became a man, I did away with childish things."

Notice that Paul said... "When I became a man, I did away with childish things..." What "things" did Paul do away with?

Let's first examine how a child acts and speaks... they are often untruthful, envious and cruel. If rebuked, they become martyrs, if crossed they are resentful and often make a scene. They are talebearers, repeating everything they hear... it's called gossip. They are given to emotional outburst and are easily puffed up. They love praise and will accept it from any source. They seek only things that appeal to self.

Do you recognize any of those characteristics in you?

Paul did!

Paul said:

"But whatever things were gain to me, those things I have counted as loss for the sake of CHRIST. More than that, I count all things to be loss in view of a surpassing value of knowing CHRIST JESUS my LORD for whom I have suffered loss of all things, and count them rubbish so that I gain Christ JESUS my Lord." (Phil. 3:7-9 NASB).

The Greek word translated gain is an accounting term meaning profit and the word for loss is also an accounting word. Paul used the language of business to describe the Spiritual transaction that occurred when Christ redeemed him. Paul is using worldly business terms to tell us it's all rubbish.

Again Paul said:

"When I became a man..." What happened when Paul finally became a man... a man with an authentic nature? He had the peace of GOD (Rom. 5:1), he knew the peace of GOD (Phil. 4:7), he rejoiced in his Spiritual children (1st Tim. 1:2), he was content in all circumstances (Phil.

4:11), he knew the only source of true strength (Phil. 4:13), he did not brood over the past, but he looked toward the future (Phil. 3:13-14), he knew GOD causes all things to work together for good (Rom 8:28), he walked victoriously in the Spirit and enjoyed abundant life.

So what does all of this mean in real terms? Paul, who was a Roman Citizen and a Pharisee, a member of the strictest, most respected Jewish sect... He was the Hebrew of all Hebrews... He had it all... Power, Prestige, Money and Education. But still considered himself a child... until he stepped across the line... then all that was once gain... he considered "Rubbish!"

Paul stepped across that line and found man's authentic nature... he began to walk in the SPIRIT, stepping out in boldness of authentic masculine courage. He knew it is one thing to have eternal life... its quite another thing to have abundant life (John 10:10), its one thing to become the righteousness of GOD in HIM (2nd Cor. 5:21), it is another thing for you to realize HIS righteousness in you (1st John 3:7), it is one thing to live in CHRIST (2nd Cor. 5:17), it is another for CHRIST to live HIS life through you (Col 1:27).

Paul said: "... But one thing I do; forgetting what lies behind and reaching forward to what lies ahead, I press on toward the goal for the prize of the upward call of GOD in CHRIST JESUS," (Phil. 3:13b-14).

JESUS said: "... I came that they might have life, and

have it abundantly!" (John 10:10).

If you do not have the abundant life that comes with authentic masculine courage you are living below what GOD has for you. Man seems to know everything about life except how to live it abundantly. All men have life, but abundant life only comes through authentic "Submission to Master."

Compelling sacrificial love is the power and authority of authentic male leadership. Without CHRIST like love active in a man's life, his leadership potential is neutralized and his GOD ordained position is void of power and influence.

But when a man recognizes that he was born to die to his flesh, to have no life of his own apart from Christ, when he joyfully chooses to live as the unique sacrifice he was designed to be... then and ONLY THEN, that same man will find the incomprehensible peace and freedom of authentic Biblical manhood.

When we began, I said I was confident if I were to sit down face-to-face, one on one with each of you... if you would open your heart... you would admit you genuinely want to walk in the authentic masculine role GOD created you to walk in. I truly believe that.

2,000 years ago Paul realized what Elijah meant when he asked all the people: (1st Kings 18:21)

"How long will you hesitate between two opinions? If the LORD is GOD Follow HIM!"

A thought JESUS echoed when HE said: (Luke 6:46)

"*Why do you call ME Lord, Lord, and not do what I say?*"

What is your answer to those questions?

Chapter Four — The Conclusion is Only the Beginning

As I pondered how to conclude this message several concepts came to mind. What could I provide you as a tool to effectuate the victorious experience of Authentic Masculine Courage GOD ordained for you? I suddenly realized the answer was so old it was new.

The Epistle of James is the "Proverbs" of the New Testament. There is no better guide to facilitate that victory. James tells men how to "Step Across the Line" from a life led by our flesh to the one led by the HOLY SPIRIT. James tells you how to be at peace in this dark depraved world.

This Epistle is not doctrinal or apologetic, it is practical. It challenges us to examine the quality of our daily lives in terms of attitudes and actions of Authentic Masculine Courage. James says a genuine faith, resulting from true repentance, will produce changes in a person's conduct and character, and the absence of change is symptomatic of dead faith... true faith cannot exist when repentance consists only of ingenious lip service.

Knowing you should already have access to the Epistle of James in your own Bible, I have purposed to reduce to writing my own thoughts of how this Epistle opened my eyes to how to be victorious in the midst of the "Conflict" Paul writes about in Philippians 1:29.

Follow me for a moment as I sojourn down memory lane. In my youth I was considered a potentially gifted athlete. But being told you have potential simply means you aren't doing it yet. Had I ever grasped the concept of getting in shape, who knows what I may have achieved? My only claim to fame is that I played High School Basketball with a legend and my good friend... "Pistol Pete" Maravich... this was such an exciting experience for me.

I'm taking the shot and Pete is headed out!

Physical conditioning required running, I didn't do running. Ironically, I greatly admired distance runners. Jim Thorpe was a boyhood hero of mine. But I was not willing to pay the price. Running was not for me. It took an auto accident when I was thirty-three to change my attitude.

Using your head as the implement of choice to remove the windshield of a car results in serious pain that does not go away overnight. You see, I have always thought of myself as that invincible, tree climbing kid. What a rude awakening when I realized my Grandfather was right, "Growing old is not for sissies!" My body hurt in places I didn't know could hurt. I was not bouncing back as I expected. I was no longer the 170lb athlete of the yesteryear... I was a sedentary 252lb couch potato. ARGH! So I did what any self-respecting, health conscious, overweight, ex-athlete would do. I joined a "Trendy" health club... telling myself, "Self, we are going to work out and GET IN SHAPE!" Who was I kidding? The hot tub, sauna, steam room and "Fruit Smoothie" machine became my exercise routine, I gained 5 lbs my first week.

While on a business trip to Dallas, some friends and I took a tour of the Cooper Aerobic Center. My curiosity peeked; I agreed to subject myself to their computerized evaluation of sports application best suited to your body structure. Imagine my shock when the computer said, "Long Distance Runner..." Their consultant informed me that my body was exceptionally proportional and designed for both efficiency and endurance. I said, "What about football, basketball, baseball, and golf... sports I like?" He politely said, "The computer doesn't make mistakes!" I thought to myself, "I have never seen a 6 foot 5 inch long distance runner... this guy is nuts!" My facial expression must have given me away... he repeated, "The computer doesn't make mistakes!"

Armed with this new information, my companions

began to chide me to join them each morning as they went jogging. Point of clarification: You jog your memory.... anything faster than a walk... is running! They persisted, undaunted by my refusals. Finally, I acquiesced and joined them. My friends lied, they did not jog! These people were certifiable, over the edge, out of control, marathon-running psychos! But to my amazement, I loved it... running was definitely my new thing. I trimmed down from 257lbs to 190lbs of lean running machine. I was hooked. I subsequently completed 5 marathons (@ 26.2 miles) and 3 full triathlons (@ 2.5 mile swim~112 mile bike~26.2 mile run). In 1982, at the ripe old age of thirty-eight, I qualified to run the "Boston Marathon" by finishing the Los Colonias Marathon in San Antonio in a time of 2 hours and 57 minutes... finishing 71st out of nearly 1,500 runners.

I became an obnoxious advocate of running. One day as I was pontificating the joys of running, a lady challenged me saying, "If running is so much fun, why do runners have a look of left over death on their faces as they run?" GOOD QUESTION! So I asked myself, "Self, shouldn't my countenance reflect my enthusiasm for the health benefits running provided?" My answer was a resounding, "YES!" From that day forward I purposed to smile from ear to ear every time I ran. To my surprise people began to noticed. Strangers would wave, blow their horns, give me the thumbs up and even yell encouragements to me! Some were so taken back by my smiling they nearly wrecked their cars!

All that brings me now to this point. If smiling as I ran could have such a radical impact on casual observers, how much more would an attitude of "considering it all joy", as I faced the various "speed bumps" in my life, have on those GOD has placed in my life to encourage and lead. If I profess to be a Christian aren't I supposed to trust GOD? Didn't JESUS say, "Why do you call ME LORD, LORD and not do what I say?" WOW! James was right, we should embrace every trial and tribulation we encounter as opportunities to grow and perfect our faith, allowing them to produce in us a character of Authentic Masculine Courage, GODly men of maturity.

We should rejoice when we aren't sure what to do, for we have a FATHER in heaven who gives generously, to those who ask, the wisdom to handle anything we may encounter. All we have to do is ask HIM, but you must ask with assurance, NO VACILLATING. GOD won't give wisdom to those who are slaves to mood swings. And GOD doesn't make us feel stupid for asking. HE loves us depending on HIM and coming to HIM for help. That's HIS job and HE does it well!

It doesn't matter if you are rich or poor the struggles come. Only GOD can get us through them. Rich or poor, have or have not we all have been given the same privilege to demonstrate our trust in GOD, the GOD of All Creation. GOD is not a respecter of worldly wealth,

HE shows HIMSELF strong to all whose heart is truly HIS.

The conflict we experience is with our own flesh, we should never say GOD is tempting us to sin. HE doesn't work that way. Temptation comes from our own inward desire to please our senses. But we are no longer in bondage to our flesh…we have been set free. We have an indwelling of the HOLY SPIRIT and HE cannot be tempted.

GOD is the provider of every good thing. Our problem is we don't see the good and we don't trust that GOD does either. My eleventh grade English teacher was the meanest, strictest, most overbearing woman I have ever known. Her class was pure torture of the cruel and unusual kind. SURELY NOTHING GOOD would ever come from this experience… NOTHING! "Who needs to learn creative writing? What a waste of time, what could I ever use that for!"

Thank you, Mrs. Farrar for caring, thank you for teaching me to put my thoughts on paper… and thank YOU GOD for knowing she would.

Hear this… GOD gave us two ears and only one mouth because HE knew it would be twice as hard to listen, as it is to talk. As HIS ambassadors we need to become better listeners. We need to be slow to speak for sure, but we also need to talk less and listen more. Becoming a better listener will help us get control of our tempers. Anger tends to distort our perception and add volume to our speech. Angry men can be quite frightening to women and children. We were designed to be a rock for them to lean on, not a rock to crush them. Our anger does not impress GOD or reflect HIS goodness.

We are not children that need to be told what's right and wrong... we know! We need to abandon all that is offensive to GOD... not just abandon it... run from it. We need to read the "Manufacturer's Handbook" (the Bible) and do all according to what is written.

GOD doesn't care if you can quote it, HE doesn't care if you can preach it, HE wants to see you live it! We read the example of the person looking in the mirror, seeing his face, and then walking away forgetting what he looked like... interesting example, but not you, right? ARE YOU SURE?

Try this... time how long it takes, next Sunday after you leave church, to BLOW IT! Your wife, kids, traffic or something will cause you to lose sight of the Man of GOD who sat in your pew, who was moved to tears by HIS word.

But, praise GOD when we walk in Authentic Masculine Courage we develop better recall. We find ourselves staying focused, we reflect HIM.

Child of GOD, to reflect HIM, we need to be real! Being "religious" doesn't cut it... and it surely doesn't mean you are GODly (does the word Pharisee come to mind?).

GODly men know how to control their mouth. If you cannot, you expose yourself to be a religious pretender.

Real GODliness, that which is pleasing to GOD, shows itself to widows and orphans and the needy, hurting people GOD brings across our path. Being a real man of GOD means you are not polluted by worldly attitudes, excuses and verbiage. Real is not shallow, real goes all the way to the core.

Being real means you don't show favoritism to those who dress well or those who can benefit you. Real demonstrates GOD's love equally to all. GOD is the one who decides the instruments HE uses... (just ask Balaam or for that matter, his donkey.) Our job is to be ready, willing and able when HE calls. You never know for sure when He may use you to touch a heart or change a life. He may not even tell you when you do... HE's like that.

Since the Epistle of James wasn't written by a disciple who followed JESUS for three years listening to HIM and being taught by HIM, the various aspects of the wisdom penned by James must have come from somewhere else... but where? It came from being mentored day by day as he grew up with JESUS.

I often find myself wondering about what James may have said or done to have JESUS impart these wonderfully insightful principles of Authentic Masculine Courage. I envision James marveling at JESUS' faithfulness to GOD's law. I can hear him saying, "JESUS, how do you remember all of GOD's commandments? How do you keep from breaking them?" JESUS probably answered, "James if you will love the LORD your GOD with all your heart, mind and strength, and love your neighbor as yourself, the rest will be a piece of cake! You wont break any of GOD's laws."

That "love your neighbor as yourself" thing, reminds me of that proverbial paraphrase, "What goes around come around!" You want tolerance, show tolerance... you want forgiveness... forgive! When I think, "You reap what you sow!" is a law of GOD. It scares me to death! I have sown some pretty bad seed in my life. Let us now pause and pray for Crop failure! Amen? Amen! AMEN!

So tell me, if it were against the law to be a Christian, could they find enough evidence to convict you? Saying you are a Christian, saying you have faith is meaningless if there is no external evidence to back it up. What good is it to tell someone you will pray for them if their need is immediate and you are the one GOD has chosen to help them? Actions speak louder than words, but sometimes our actions are so loud our words can't be heard.

Saying there is a GOD is a NO BRAINER! That is not an expression of faith. The demons know there is a GOD and are smart enough to tremble with fear. Most people, who profess to be Christians today, live their lives mocking GOD. But that's just this ole cowboy preacher's opinion. Jesus probably wasn't serious about that "you are either for ME or against ME" thing. I probably read way too much into that statement. Nah, on second thought, I think HE meant every word. There's no middle of the road with JESUS and fence straddling doesn't cut it! GOD wants REAL and HE wants it now! Anything short of 100% is just smoke and mirrors. GOD doesn't settle for most... HE wants ALL. The only ones deceived by playing church are the actors.

Brothers, you need to really pray about whether you have been called to be a teacher. Do not assume that role casually.

Both GOD and man will hold you to a higher standard. GOD expects a good and faithful steward and man just delights in finding fault. Being a teacher requires a total commitment and skin thick as a rhino's. There is too much of what is called "burn-out' in church leadership these days. And frankly I don't understand how you can get burnt out doing what GOD called you to do. My Grandma Graham was probably right when she observed about most preachers, "They weren't sent, they just went!"

This is tough but you need to hear it... it seems the hardest thing for a man to learn is when to just SHUT UP! If you can learn to control your mouth your whole life will change. Man has figured out how to fly in space, walk on the moon, control large ships with a small rudder, he controls large majestic horses with a small bit in their mouth, but he can't seem to figure out how to just SHUT UP! Our goal should be to get control of that tongue and reprogram the brain behind it to speak only that which edifies GOD. I read somewhere, "Out of the abundance of the heart the mouth speaks!" Your mouth is the key. If you can control that, you will walk victoriously. It is just that black and white. If I gave you an orange and asked you to squeeze it with all your strength... what would come out? Juice, right? Tomato juice? NO! Apple juice? NO! Orange juice would come out because it is an orange. My point is this, when you are squeezed by the adversities in your life, who comes out? Like in the story of Shadrach, Mesach, and Abednego; do those looking in your fire see JESUS? Or when you get squeezed does a foul mouth, loud, abusive jerk come out screaming and railing at everyone in your path... or is it the hurt little boy pouting, sulking, and feeling sorry for himself that comes out... or should I ask the woman in your life that question? To whatever degree, positive or negative, whoever comes out is who you really are! That other guy is just someone who you pretend to be when things are going well.

But praise GOD, there is GOOD NEWS! We don't have to stay stuck on stupid! The orange will always be the orange, but we can change. It is a fact that God loves you just as you are, but HE loves you too much to let you stay that way. The Holy Spirit knows just how hot the fire needs to be to burn out the trash! And HE is faithful!

When we truly find ourselves seeking GOD's face, relying on HIS HOLY SPIRIT to lead us, we will no longer feel the need to compare circumstances of others to ourselves. We will be secure in who HE says we are.

The argument and struggles we find ourselves embroiled in are the result of the self-centered competitive nature of the "old man." His desires to assert himself over others, his insidious fear and his apathy have been washed away.

The "old man" is DEAD! If we will just leave him buried, we will find ourselves freed from concerns of what others think. Our envy and jealousy will fade away and we won't strive for the recognition of man. We will be at peace knowing we find favor with GOD.

Our hearts will be filled with GODly desires and we will no longer find ourselves asking for things with wrong motives. We will lack nothing because HE meets ALL our needs.

Okay, here I go again, what did James do to make JESUS explain that friendship with the world was hostility toward GOD? "All right", picture this, James comes home from Hebrew School one day, rapping "Hava Nagila," his turban on backwards, he's wearing a size 4XL tunic, his sandals are untied, and he's got a big gold Star of David and a huge gold chain around his neck… he slides sideways into the room and says, "What it is homie?" JESUS, somewhat puzzled says, "James, what's with this new look?" To wit James replies, as he moonwalks across the carpentry shop, "YO, Oui Vey Bro! This is how all my homeboys are stylin' down on the mall! Know what I am saying man?" JESUS, kneeling to tie James' sandals says, "James, James, James don't you know that to be a friend of the world is to be an enemy of GOD? And your Mama is not going to be happy... and when your Mama's not happy, nobody is happy!" All right! That's a stretch... but it could have happened!

You have a wonderful live-in tutor, mentor and friend residing, abiding and indwelling within you... HE jealously longs to have an intimate, lasting fellowship with you. HE waits eagerly to shower you with HIS grace to handle any and all circumstances. You need only to humble yourself and receive it. GOD resists your pride but gives GRACE to your humility.

Let's take a moment to look at this word Grace that we use so casually. Most church people will tell you grace is "God's unmerited favor or help," which is Webster's definition. Strong's says the word we translate grace in the New Testament is a Greek word, which defined, is: "God's divine influence on the heart that reflects in the life." WOW! That's a lot more poignant than unmerited favor, wouldn't you agree? I believe it delineates the profundity GOD truly meant HIS GRACE to have.

And, when through grace, we rely on the Holy Spirit we are in submission to GOD. That means we are washed by the Blood and empowered to resist the devil. James says, "Submit to GOD..." Okay, I did that! "Resist the devil..." okay, define resist! This time Webster's and

Strong's pretty much agree. First, resist does not mean fighting or railing… the word is passive. Resist defined is, "To prevent a particular action (as a coating)." It is that sidebar in parenthesis that caught my eye. Strong's says coating; covering and atonement are all from the same root word. So if resist is, "as a coating" and Noah was told by GOD to "coat" the Ark to make it resistant to outside elements, and we have been coated with the Blood of Jesus… hmmm? I GET IT! We have been "Holy Spirit Scotch Guarded!" Satan can't penetrate it; he rolls off like water off a duck. GOD says, "Resist the devil and he will just roll off!" I love that visual image! It gives a brand new meaning to the term, "losing your grip!" Satan has lost his grip… I love it!

By "grasping" the concept that Satan has "no grip" you have let go that which encumbered you and embraced that which empowers you to draw closer to GOD. And GOD is faithful when we draw closer to HIM, HE will draw closer to us. But understand the closer you get to the Light the more your flaws are exposed and the more you will be convicted of how worthless you are without HIM. But here's where HIS GRACE does it again. Did you know it is impossible to experience guilt in the presence of absolute unconditional forgiveness and love? Once you rid yourself of guilt you can focus on being the man, husband, father and friend you were designed by GOD to be.

And, what is with all these "Grandiose Plans" we make without praying or seeking GOD first? Since we don't know if we even have a tomorrow, doesn't it strike you as prudent to consult the ONE who does know? You know that is the right thing to do, so why don't you do it? HE says, "Knowing what is right and not doing it is a sin!"

I for one have spent far too much of my life being impressed by my Rolex, my Mercedes, my wife's Jaguar and all the money we made. None of which had any lasting or eternal value. Solomon summed it all best, "its all vanity and chasing the wind!"

As I patiently look toward our Savior's return, I am convinced that I want to be found working... I don't want to waste even a minute. The only path I want to travel is the narrow path Jesus speaks of. It's a narrow path with no room for Satan. I'm on a bicycle built for two, Jesus is up front leading the way and I'm on the back, enjoying the ride!

My daughter Hope told me one day, "Dad, Jesus may have turned water into wine, but HE won't turn whining into nothing!" She added, "Whining wastes time you could use praising GOD!" She was only six at the time... she is just like her Mom, smart and beautiful!

The Bible is replete with examples of God's grace and mercy. HE never abandons us. HE is always holding us in the hollow of HIS hand. I can hear HIM whispering, "IT'LL BE ALL RIGHT!"

Once again let me stress that your mouth speaks volumes to who you are. Your yes should be yes and your no should be no! You should never make promises you can't or won't keep. Wouldn't it be awesome if Christian men had the reputation of truly being honest, hard working and reliable? I would love to see billboards and ads by fortune 500 companies reading, "NOW HIRING! CHRISTIAN MEN PREFERRED! If only we had a nation of GOD fearing men walking in Authentic Masculine Courage, talking with GOD not talking at HIM. What a concept!

Prayer is so powerful when truly understood. The purpose of prayer is not to inform GOD of anything, GOD knows all things. Prayer is your opportunity to express your submission to GOD's sovereignty and your trust in HIS faithfulness. The diligent sincere prayer of a man experiencing Authentic Masculine Courage prevails in all circumstances, because first and foremost it honors GOD. And there are two times you need to pray. When you want to and when you don't. You should pray whenever and wherever the Spirit leads you. Pray boldly without concern as to what others may say or think. You should sing HIS praises always. My beloved Catherine and daughter Hope act like they don't know me sometimes because I will breakout in song anytime, anywhere, in the grocery store, bank, gas station, anytime anywhere the Spirit moves.

Friends, admittedly there are times when you will become weary. Times when it seems your prayers are merely bouncing off the roof of your mouth. Weariness comes from unmet expectations. It comes when your focus shifts from trusting GOD's plan, to wanting GOD to do it your way. GOD's word says, "Hope deferred makes the heart sick. But desire fulfilled is a tree of life." That proverb addresses the realization that when man's expectations are not met, it makes your heart weary. But when GOD's plan comes to fruition, and His plan is going to come to fruition, it breathes new life into your heart. You must obediently refocus your attention of GOD's intrinsic goodness and that HE declares that HE has a plan for you, a plan for your good, not your harm, a plan to give you a future and a hope. But with your expectations comes failure, with failure comes separation, with separation comes loneliness, with loneliness come despair and thus weariness. And this is where men coming together in one confident accord are most effective. When your heart is heavy, when weakness blurs your vision and your frustrations get out of hand, seek out men of Authentic Masculine Courage and ask them to take you to the throne of GRACE. As they lift you up, you will be reminded you have never been forsaken, you are not facing this struggle alone. Acknowledge your weariness and trust the plan of GOD and like Shadrach, Mesach, and Abednego you will be delivered from the flames of your own weariness. GOD is faithful.

There is a tremendous power in men of GOD holding each other up as Aaron and Hur did Moses. It brings forth victory. You must be willing to be accountable unto death, the death of your flesh and the death of your expectations. Through Authentic Masculine Courage you are free to truly experience genuine sacrificial, CHRIST-like love that love covers a multitude of flaws and empowers you to keep your feet on the path GOD has set before you. The journey begins with a single step, it's time to step up and step out.

"Authentic Masculine Courage is a man willingly setting aside his temporal expectations and accepting GOD's word that He has a plan, a man facing his fear and choosing obedience!" – Onesimus, Circa 2007

Paul chose obedience and stepped across that line. I have made my decision and stepped across that line as well. I challenge you today to take that strong, courageous step. It is a step that leaves everything on the altar, it takes GOD at HIS word and doesn't ask any questions, it trusts HIM no matter how ominous circumstances seem. It is a step of FAITH that says, "GOD is working out HIS perfect will in my life and I CAN WAIT, I CAN ENDURE and I WILL OVERCOME!

Let's lift our hands and our hearts to the LORD and ask HIM to have HIS way with us and in us today and always. Let a paraphrase of Paul's own words become implanted in our hearts and minds as they truly come to fruition in *us today.*

"Therefore because I am now in Christ and Christ is now in me, I am a new Creature; the old things have passed away; behold, new things have come!" (2nd Corinthians 5:17)

As GOD has shown us through these majestic horses and their demonstration of rebellion in chapter one... until the decision is made to cross the line from our way to HIS way our lives will never become useful... like the horse we will have no authentic purpose... we will flounder in a lake of inadequacy, trapped behind a dam of deception. That dam is a lie put forth by Satan... let's choose today to walk in TRUTH... leaving the man we were behind and finding authentic masculine courage in

HIM as we step across the line.

These are the words of my Grandma Graham's favorite old hymn...

"Rise up, O men of GOD!
Have done with lesser things,
Give heart, and soul, and mind and strength
To serve the King of Kings.
Rise up, O men of GOD!
The church for you does wait,
Her strength unequal to her task,
Rise up and make her great!"

Again Child of GOD, it will take courage... John Wayne defined courage as, "Being scared to death and saddling up anyway!" Choose to "saddle up" today... let's ride off into GOD's sunset... and be the men HE ordained us to be!

Hi, my name is Jonah... and trust me... when *GOD* calls you, you're going to mind... sooner or later... you're going to mind! You are going to do it *HIS* way... one way or another... now or later!

MY PHOTOS

Catherine and Pastor Jim

Pastor Jim

Former Texas Ranger Foundation Member

Jim and Catherine out riding their horses and looking

DR. JIM VON SCHOUNMACHER

beautiful in their matching U.S.A shirts

SUBMISSION TO MASTER
IN SEARCH OF MAN'S AUTHENTIC NATURE

Jim and Catherine VonSchounmacher
The Founding Directors of MorningStar Ranch Ministries

Fifteen years ago, MorningStar Ranch started as a small non-profit ministry using animals to help troubled families and at risk youth grow in both confidence and in GOD's Spirit. Over the year's, your generosity has allowed us to move to a permanent location just south west of San Antonio, Texas.

The ministry now includes horses, llamas, pot-bellied pigs, pygmy goats, alpacas, chickens, ducks and much, much more... all co-existing peacefully in a setting on our own little 30 acre piece of Texas. MorningStar Ranch is completely supported by those who are moved to help further GOD's Word through the ministry of animals. Completely operated by donations and volunteers, your tax deductible donation will help further GOD's work throughout the coming year.

Visit online at http://www.morningstarranch.org or write for more information to; MorningStar Ranch Ministries, 226 Cutting Horse Lane, Somerset, Texas 78069

NOTES

NOTES

NOTES

Made in the USA
Columbia, SC
15 June 2022

61760887R00071